Seven out of Ten

Missing
Fishhooks

Will Eventually
Be Found in an
Angler's Thumb

~~~~~~~~~~

Sandy Lindsey

A Fishing Humor Book

Andrews McMeel
Publishing
Kansas City

www.andrewsmcmeel.com

98 99 00 01 02 BAM 10 9 8 7 6 5 4 3 2 1

Library of Congress Cataloging-in-Publication Data
Lindsey, Sandy
    Seven out of ten missing fishhooks will eventually be found in an angler's thumb: a fishing humor book / Sandy Lindsey.
       p. cm.
    ISBN: 0-8362-5209-8 (pbk.)
    1. Fishing—humor. I. Title.
PN6231.F5L56   1998
818'.5402—dc21   97-36642
                                                  CIP

Design by Lee Fukui

To my husband, Bill,
who lured me into fishing.

Contents

"If you can't laugh at fishing,
you can't laugh at anything."

SOPHOCLES "SKUNKED AGAIN" THE GREEK

Seven out of Ten
Missing
Fishhooks
Will Eventually
Be Found in an
Angler's Thumb

10 Clues That Fishing Has Taken Over Your Life

1. During boring meetings at the office, you practice tying knots under the table.

2. You started a write-in campaign to nominate George Poveromo's video *Successful Bait Rigging* for an Academy Award.

3. You turned your bathtub into a giant livewell so that you can go out for a few days ahead of a big tournament and stock up on bait fish.

4. If you had your way, you'd decorate the family Christmas tree with plugs, chuggers, jigs, and flies.

5. Instead of snoring, your wife/girlfriend/dog says that your mouth mimics fish lips all night long.

6. You plan on naming your future children Penn, Ande, Stren, and Star-brite.

7. Your wardrobe consists mainly of T-shirts purchased at fishing seminars.

8. You've cleaned out the kitchen pantry and now use it to store your lures, color coded by shelf.

9. You eat chili out of the can with a Drone spoon from which you have removed the hook.

10. Every week you submit a new entry to the Fishing Hall of Shame. (And you're getting quite upset that they continue to deny you admission.)

10 Common Fishing Terms Explained

Catch and Release

The act of tossing excess fish overboard right before the local fish and game officer pulls over a boat that has caught over its limit.

Hook

(1) A curved piece of metal used to catch fish. (2) A clever advertisement to entice a fisherman to spend his life savings on a new rod and reel. (3) The punch administered by said fisheman's wife after he spends their life savings on new tackle (see also Right Hook, Left Hook).

Line

Something you give your coworkers when they ask on Monday how your fishing went the past weekend.

Lure

An object that is semienticing to fish, but will drive an angler into such a frenzy that he will charge his credit card to the limit before exiting the tackle shop.

Reel

A weighted object that causes a rod to sink quickly when dropped overboard.

Rod

An attractively painted length of fiberglass that keeps an angler from ever getting too close to a fish.

School

A grouping in which fish are taught to avoid your $29.99 lures and hold out for Spam instead.

Tackle

What your last catch did to you as you reeled him in, but just before he wrestled free and jumped back overboard.

Tackle Box

A box shaped alarmingly like your comprehensive first-aid kit. Only a tackle box contains many sharp objects, so that when you reach into the wrong box blindly to get a Band-Aid, you soon find that you need more than one.

Test

(1) The amount of strength a fishing line affords an angler when fighting fish in a specific weight range. (2) A measure of your creativity in blaming "that damn line" for once again losing the fish.

Things Fishermen Don't Ever Want to Hear

"You know that huge fish you just let get away?
I've got him on my line now."

"I thought *you* were bringing the beer."

"I'm afraid the engine repair isn't going to be
as simple as we first thought."

"Your tackle box is back at the dock."

"The dead bait is moving."

"Have you had a doctor look at that ugly
sun spot on the back of your neck?"

"Don't worry, we'll figure out what's wrong
with your outboard."

"I think the word you're looking for is skunked, you know, down for the count, 0 for 10, struck out, bombed..."

"I don't know if we have enough gas to make it back to the weigh-in."

"Where could that rod we were just trolling with have gone?"

"I think my line is tangled with yours—again."

"Can you leave the boat here at the shop for a few more days? We're getting much closer to diagnosing the real problem."

"You don't mind if I use roadkill instead of a more traditional bait, do you?"

"Sorry you didn't catch any fish today. You can have one of mine. I've got more than enough."

"I just drank the last beer."

"I know it seems like it's taken forever to fix your boat, but don't worry, we're not going to charge you for dry storage. However, you do owe us for...and...and...and..."

From a male fishing partner: "I just wanted you to know that I think of you as much, much more than just a fishing buddy."

Fishlife

	The Ideal Fishing Trip	**Reality**
7 A.M.	Depart from the dock. The weather is perfect. The water is perfect. Your cooler is filled with your favorite chilled beer.	You get to the dock only to realize that you left the boat keys at home. (Return home. Do Not Pass Go. Do Not Collect $200.)
8 A.M.	You've caught your first fish of the day and it's a beauty. You start planning the guest list for tonight's fish fry.	Back at the dock with keys in hand: An ominous dark cloud passes overhead. You open your cooler to find that the lid wasn't shut tight and your beer is getting warm. You stiffen your resolve and head out anyway.

	The Ideal Fishing Trip	**Reality**
8:30 A.M.	Fish numbers two and three also go on the grill tonight to feed the guests. Fish numbers four and five will go in your brother's fridge because you feel compelled to share the wealth—and gloat over your catches.	Currents are strong and keep pushing you away from your favorite fishing hole. You take this personally and mutter foul words as you swill warm beer.
10:30 A.M.	You begin your usual program of "catch and release" after filling your livewell with enough fish for your immediate family and nearest neighbors for a week. The next cold beer is well deserved.	You finally get a big fish on and after thirty minutes of earnest fighting, it runs off with the one-of-a-kind, never-fail, handmade $25 lure that your brother-in-law gave you for Christmas.
Noon	Lunch break. You open the cooler your loving wife packed and take out an overstuffed sandwich. You smile	Lunch break. You open the cooler and discover that your bologna-and-mustard sandwich from 7-Eleven has

The Ideal Fishing Trip	Reality
to yourself at the thought that if oven-roasted turkey wasn't to your liking, you definitely have the makings of some great sushi swimming around you.	become water-logged from the melting ice. You toss it overboard in disgust. It is caught by the same fish that stole your lure.
1:00 P.M. Tenth fish. You keep this one because you think it might be a state record.	Your skin begins to redden (guess who forgot sunblock?) as the flat, hot beer begins to taste good.
2:00 P.M. You take a moment to watch the birds fly around you and commune with nature.	You decide to move to a more productive spot. The engine won't start—your batteries are dead.
3:00 P.M. Catch and release three more prize fish, then take a break to snack on a slice of homemade pecan pie.	Get a jump start from another boat. Limp to a new fishing spot.

	The Ideal Fishing Trip	**Reality**
4:00 P.M.	Get that one final fish, then head home to invite some friends over and fire up the grill.	Call on the radio for help. Pay $300 to be towed back to the dock.
5:00 P.M.	At the dock, you find out that you were correct—one of your fish is a potential state record.	Cringe as you hear the estimated repair bill. Spend what money you have left at a fish market on a decent fish to show to the smug always-successful fisherman who lives next door to you.
6:00 P.M.	Fish fry: Good food. Good company. Your backyard looks like one of those "partying with a large group of close friends" beer commercials.	You toss your meager fish on a lonely grill. None of your friends are available to come over, they're all at the large party next door. Their festive chatter soon begins to get on your nerves and you go inside, muttering about living next to a "darned beer commercial."

The Ideal
Fishing Trip

Reality

9:00 P.M. After cleaning your grill, you take a moment to stare at stars twinkling above and sigh. Today was certainly some day.

After cleaning your grill, you take a moment to stare at stars twinkling above and sigh. Today was certainly some day.

What a Master Angler Will Never Tell You About Attracting Fish

1. The primary purpose of expensive fishing lures is to separate a fisherman from his wallet. Attracting fish is secondary.

2. Seven out of ten misplaced hooks will eventually be found in an angler's thumb.

3. Most lures fall into one of two categories: (1) The lures that a fisherman swears he swears by and that he will generously share with you, and (2) The ones that he hides because they really work.

4. The reason the spoon is such a popular lure is its versatility, which allows an angler to successfully go after a large variety of freshwater and saltwater fish. In a pinch it will also

function as a primitive beer can opener when the pop-top breaks off.

5. Lucky Charms cereal will work as well as some of the most sophisticated flies. Especially the marshmallow hearts and stars.

6. In addition to using lead shot to weight your lures, you can also put lead shot in the fish you catch just prior to putting the fish on a scale, to impress your friends with its "improved" weight. (Note: This is grounds for justifiable homicide during a bass tournament.)

7. Ideally, the best sinkers are wide enough and heavy enough to knock out a large fish so that he floats unconscious to the surface and you can avoid all the mess and fuss normally associated with reeling him in.

8. A grenade can be useful when trying to free a snagged lure.

9. When on a fishing vacation, always remember: No matter what the locals will tell you, and how much they charge for the tip, the only *guaranteed* places to find fish are listed in the Yellow Pages under "Fish Markets."

Fanatic Fisherman Test Work vs. Bass

1. When you want to take the day off and go fishing you:

    a. Call in sick.

    b. Call in dead.

    c. Call in a bomb threat to your office building.

2. When your boss insists you come in despite your claim that you have the bubonic plague:

    a. Spend the day kissing up to your boss—after all, this is your weekly paycheck that we're talking about.

    b. Paint green spots all over yourself and cough on any coworkers who are foolish enough to come near you.

    c. Take out a shotgun and clean it prominently at your desk, until your boss agrees that you do look a bit peaked and probably should go home.

3. When you don't have a project completed on time because you spent the morning going after the big one who always gets away, you:

   a. Blame it on your coworkers.

   b. Blame it on your computer.

   c. Set your computer on fire and claim that your work was lost in the resulting meltdown.

4. When your boss takes you aside and confidentially says that he believes fishing is affecting your work performance, you:

   a. Agree with him patronizingly, then, when he isn't looking, sneak out the back door to where you've hidden your trailered boat.

   b. Agree to see a psychiatrist about your problem, then have your fishing partner send in bills as Ira Angler, M.D

   c. Use your boss for chum.

5. If you got the chance to take a round-the-world fishing excursion, in order to pay for it, you would:

   a. Sell your car and home.

   b. Sell off company office furniture and supplies while your boss is out of town.

c. Sell the company you work for by having your boss sign a sale agreement when he thinks he's signing your resignation.

RESULTS: Give yourself 5 points for each "a" answer, 3 points for each "b," and 1 point for each "c" response. If you scored 20–25 points you are a compulsive liar, which makes us believe that you are probably a decent fisherman (or so you'd tell us while using your highly developed prevarication skills); 10–20 points—you've got more than your share of social dysfunction (if you spent as much energy working as you do trying to get out of it, you'd own your own company by now and be able to take off whenever you wanted); 5–10 points— you are a true fishing psychopath who'll be happy to learn that your terrified coworkers have started a petition for your boss to allow you to fish your favorite secret fishing hole every day.

More Things a Fisherman Doesn't Ever Want to Hear

"Hey, isn't that your ex-wife over there
in your new bass boat?"

"I thought *you* were listening when they
gave us the directions at the dock."

"The dog is stealing fish out of the livewell."

"Doesn't that guy swimming toward our boat
look exactly like the guy who was on
America's Most Wanted last night?"

"Uh-oh, I think I accidentally turned off
the baitwell a while back."

"Do we have a minute to stop by the
detox center on the way to the dock?"

"Do we have any penicillin on board?"

"Can live bait be resuscitated after it's been floating at the top of the tank for a half hour?"

"Your new rod just went overboard."

"We can use your wife's water skis as oars and paddle back."

"I think our live bait has just turned into stinkbait."

"Do you have good insurance on this boat?"

Things You Should Never Say at a Strange Tackle Shop

"All right, who's going to be a sport and show
me their favorite fishing hole?"

"Anyone know who owns the red pickup
out front that I just hit?"

About the shop's merchandise:
"Look at all this antique tackle."

"Let me tell you about a fish I once caught..."

"What! No high-tech lures?
How can you people catch anything?"

"One of you has got to be named Bubba...
let me guess."

"You do take traveler's checks, don't you?"

"Your rods look as if they were wrapped at the Lighthouse Project for the Blind."

About a picture hung behind the cash register:
"Are those some ugly fish you caught or
is that a family portrait?"

"I only use imported hooks."

"I need a new rod. Do you have anything
in blue to match my reel?"

When a woman walks into the shop:
"Want to see my lure?"

And never, ever say:

"You call this live bait?
Why, in New York we..."
(You won't get any further than that.)

Politically Correct Fishing

The following is an updated and thoroughly revised list of angling terms in keeping with the politically correct nature of the 1990s:

Skunked	Catch challenged
Artificial lure	Recyclable bait
Fish	Marine resident
Losing a fish	Catch and release
Bait casting	Bait and release
Fisherman	Angling afflicted
Fly fisherman	Obsessive-compulsive sufferer

Chum	Marine compost
Fishing guide	Piscatorial engineer
Female fishing guide	Piscatorial engineer (formerly: gal or babe)
Hook	Fish-securing device
Reel	Dinner-fish retrieval mechanism
Fishing license	A permit that allows an angler to leave a certain number of lures on the bottom each day without fear of upsetting the local marine ecosystem or violating EPA regulations.

How to Tell if You're More of a Fisherman Than a Family Man

1. You can't remember your own children's names, but you can give exact details about the drag system on every reel you've ever owned.

2. You remember your wedding anniversary each year only because it falls on the same day you bought your boat.

3. You tried to legally change the family name to Penn, after your favorite reel. (Unfortunately, the fishing-tackle manufacturer had trade-marked it first.)

4. You outfitted the family cat with a scuba tank and snorkel so that you could toss her overboard and have her checkout potential fishing locations.

5. You once tried to use your mother-in-law as a sinker.

6. You accidentally used your son's worm-farm science project as bait.

7. For Christmas last year you gave each of your children a complete set of 1/0 to 9/0 hooks and a Donmar hollow-edge hook sharpener.

8. Your fishing tackle has its own room, while your three children share a bedroom.

9. You replaced the Mickey Mouse mobile that hung above your baby's cradle with one made out of Cotee jigs.

10. You carve the family Thanksgiving turkey with a Normark fillet knife.

10 More Common Fishing Terms Explained

Chum

(1) Chopped-up fish, guts, and other edibles tossed overboard to attract fish. (2) A fishing buddy, who if he catches one more of "your" fish today, will become number 1 above.

Clicker

A noisemaker added to a reel so that you'll know when you finally do get a hit, long after you've fallen asleep, but not in time to set the hook before the fish gets away.

Custom Reel Casing

A simple way to improve the performance of a standard reel without incurring the expense associated with buying a newer, more complex model. It will usually keep an angler from feeling the need for said complete new setup for approximately thirty days, or until the next Penn sale, whichever comes first.

Fishing Lore

An extremely nonsensical fishing tip that made it around the globe twice and has since spawned the manufacture of countless useless lures and accessories, and now has its own *New York Times* best-selling book on the subject.

Handmade Lures

Uniquely designed lures made in some old guy's garage, which are so effective that you'll pay $50 a piece for them. The following week the old-timer sells the design to Luhr Jensen who improves upon it and begins to mass manufacture them for $3.50 each.

Homemade Spoon

A virtually foolproof lure shaped very similar to your wife's recently missing earrings.

Jig

(1) A lure made up of a weighted, often shiny metal head, and a feather or some other type of tried-and-true fish-attracting material. (2) A dance a barefoot angler does after stepping on the hook he just dropped.

Lead Shot

A weight used to sink a lure or bait to a desired depth. Infrequently used by unscrupulous tournament fishermen to increase the weight of their catch, which can, in turn, lead to them being shot with Remington lead.

Solitude

(1) The joy of having the perfect fishing hole all to yourself (2) Having your radio die just as you are about to call Channel 16 for help.

Tag and Release

An involuntary action that is similar to the children's game of tag, in that you get to momentarily touch a fish, but before you can yell "You're it," the slippery fish is off to hide once again.

Unorthodox Things You Can Do to Enhance Your Fishing Boat Security

1. Circle your boat with yellow "Crime Scene—Do Not Cross" tape and trace the chalk outline of a fallen body on deck.

2. Don't organize your boat after a day's fishing. The average criminal will mistake the mess for a vessel that has already been ransacked.

3. Leave out a key and detailed directions to a bigger, newer, better-equipped boat that's nearby.

4. Create a mannequin of a thief, such as you would a more traditional Halloween scarecrow, and place him on board to deter any subsequent criminals.

5. Surround the boat with visible trip wires, which when tripped activate a tape recording of a bomb ticking.

6. Stencil "Property of the _____ County Sheriff's Department" prominently on your hull, or casually leave a worn sheriff's shirt hanging over the back of the driver's seat.

7. Scatter fake bloodstains around on deck.

8. Post any or all of the following signs: Condemned, Seized Property of the DEA, Hazardous Waste Aboard, Warning: Asbestos Present.

9. Leave last week's fishing catch on board. (Note: There is one side effect to using this method of theft deterrent—you won't want to go back on board either.)

You Know You're Going to Have a Bad Day of Fishing When...

The clouds above you darken ominously, the
waters about you rise, and the sea parts!

You pass your boss on another boat.
The same boss you told earlier that day
that you were sick.

Your bait is larger than any fish you encounter.

Your guide boasts about how lucky he is
to have been promoted from boat detailer to
substitute guide in just two short weeks.

Your doctor tracks you down via the marine
radio to inform you that he has a bit of bad
news about your most recent test results.

Your brother-in-law, who has gone fishing with
you, suddenly starts referring to his wife, your
sister, as your next-of-kin.

Your fishing buddy asks if you were supposed to fill the gas tank or if he was. (Of course, the answer is "he was.")

The local authorities stop you, and believing that your live bait is your catch, ticket you for keeping undersize fish.

You spot your ex-wife, who when you two were married hated fishing, standing on the deck of a brand-new bass boat next to her new husband and catching all the big ones.

More Clues That You're an Obsessed Fisherman

1. You live in a $400-a-month apartment, fish from a $45,000 boat, and over the past ten years have spent over $200,000 in rods, reels, bait, and lures.

2. You floss your teeth with #4 Momoi Flourocarbon line.

3. You practiced and mastered 147 different casting techniques before you found out that slow trolling works best for the majority of fish you go after.

4. You dumped your last girlfriend after you found out that when she said she had "great influence with the Zodiac people," she was talking about astrology and not the inflatables manufacturer.

5. You have a lifetime pass for the world's largest boat show in Fort Lauderdale.

6 When your wife nagged you for a hot tub, you installed a 300-gallon Chem-Tainer tank instead so that it could double as a live-bait holding tank before a big tournament. (Which works out just fine since, as it turns out, your wife isn't as enthused about the "hot tub" idea now as she was before you put it in.)

7. When it was your turn to cook dinner you used Culprit scented worms and salamanders as a salad garnish (and were never asked to cook again).

8. You store your favorite cap in a PerfectCurve brim shaper to keep it ready for the day when you catch your IGFA record fish and take the photo with it that will appear on your Christmas cards forever.

9. On an average week, you see the local fish and game officer more than you see your kids. Unless, of course, the kids have gone fishing with you.

10. On an average day, your kids can outfish you three to one with their Snoopy rods and reels. Which is why they don't go fishing with you more often.

The Family Fishing-
Boat Budget: A Male and
Female Perspective

Your "Boat Budget"		Your Wife's "Boat Budget"	
New wide-screen deluxe four-color fish finder	$500	Food for your four children	$500
Repair hole in hull	$300	School clothes for the kids	$300
Baitwell upgrades	$150	Lunch money for youngest kids	$150
New deck carpeting	$450	Baby-sitter fees for a year	$450
New rods and reels	$800	Rent	$800

Your "Boat Budget"		Your Wife's "Boat Budget"	
		New work clothes for your wife who will now be going back to work to	
Monthly beer allowance	$200	help pay off the boat loan	$200
Monthly gas allowance	$300	Airfare for her mother's annual visit	$300
High-tech lures	$200	Food for her mother's visit	$200
Miscellaneous snacks, etc.	$75	Monthly all-inclusive boat allowance	$75

Fish Facts

1. A boonie hat makes a great lure holder. (But watch out for the hooks...oops, too late.)

2. Your wife's earrings will attract more fish than the most high-tech lure any day.

3. Mounting a working cannon on your bow will assure you a good space at even the most crowded fishing holes.

4. Bringing along your pet boa constrictor will yield the same results when fishing in a stream.

5. It will rain every day throughout your fishing vacation, with the sun coming out and shining brightly as you return to the dock on your final day.

6. The amount of water resistance afforded by most marine electronics is in direct proportion to the number of days left in the warranty.

7. The person who invented insect repellent had a sick sense of humor.

8. The goal of fishing is to catch a fish that weighs more than the combined weight of the rod, reel, lure, and beer intake required to boat the fish.

Bumper Stickers for Fishing Boats

Ever wondered what would happen if the average fisherman suddenly took a page out of the *Official RV Owners Handbook* and began to slap countless bumper stickers on their transom? Were that the case, the following are some thoughts on the sentiments that you might find floating along beside you:

No, this is not an abandoned boat.

We're staying together for the sake of our Hatteras.

If a boater's money could talk, all it would say is good-bye.

I don't lie, cheat or steal...except when fishing.

My other boat is a Viking.

The worst day boating is better than the best day at the office.

Happiness is seeing the photo of the guy
who beat you at last year's bass tournament
on a milk carton.

No, my boat hasn't appeared in
an episode of the *X-Files*.

Is there life before the tournament start gun?

Life's too short to spend your weekends on land.

No radio. Already stolen.

I break for bass.

I speed up for jet skiers.

It's lonely at the top...of my four-story
tuna tower.

My ex-wife's boat is a broom.

Mother-in-law in anchor locker.

My kid can outfish your honor student.

Naked waterskiing instructor. Free lessons.

Stop honking, I'm paddling as fast as I can.

My wife says that if I go fishing one more time,
she's going to leave me....I sure am going
to miss her.

10 More Common Fishing Terms Explained

Angler

An obsessed individual who owns a house that is falling down due to neglect, a truck whose color can best be described as Rust-Oleum, and a pristine boat that he chammies down methodically before and after each trip.

Knot

(1) An insecure connection between your hook and fishing line. (2) A permanent tangle on your spinning reel that forces you to go out and buy a bigger, better, much more expensive rig.

Landing Net

A net used to help drag a large wiggling fish, or an inebriated fishing buddy, on board.

Live Bait

The biggest fish you'll handle all day.

Quiet Water

Your surroundings after you stop cursing your bad luck and fall asleep at the reel.

Skunked Fisherman

One who returns to the boat ramp many, many hours after his buddies have gone home so that there are no witnesses to his catch or lack thereof.

Sinker

(1) A weight attached to a lure to get it to the bottom. (2) The nickname of your boat.

Thumb

A temporary hook holder.

Treble Hook

Triples the odds of your catching a fish. Quadruples the odds of your getting the hook caught in your thumb (see above).

Trolling

What you do after you've lost a $500 rod-and-reel setup overboard.

"Are We out of Beer Again?!! I Can't Take It Anymore!!!"

(8 Ways to Tell if You're Suffering from Fishermen's Stress Syndrome)

1. You feel a gnawing pain in your stomach each time a fish gnaws at your bait while leaving the hook untouched.

2. You only bring beer along on a fishing trip because you can't get your teeth unclenched long enough to consume a solid lunch.

3. You don't blink while you have a fish on the line.

4. Instead of searching out a newer, better lure, you go off in search of a new flavor of Maalox.

5. Your fishing dog brings along a white flag and keeps it at hand for when you lose another fish and your emotions erupt.

6. You've heard somewhere that laughter is the antithesis of stress and are determined to try it. (Note: Laughing at a fishing buddy who has been skunked again will cause his stress level to rise considerably. So make sure he has put his fillet knife and other sharp objects away before expressing your mirth.)

7. You can't wait to get your hands on those people who say that music counteracts stress and introduce them to your fishing buddy who whistles and/or hums constantly from the minute you leave the dock to the minute you return.

8. At the end of yet another day of fruitless fishing, warm Pepto-Bismol tastes almost as good as a cold beer.

The Biggest Lies
Fishermen Tell

"I'm sure I've got my fishing license here somewhere, officer."

"The monster was huge, I tell you, huge."

"My wife doesn't mind what I spend on fishing."

"You buy the beer today, I'll bring it next time."

"I don't know how those undersized fish got into my livewell, officer."

"I'd never lie to you."

"This boat can go at least another fifty miles when she says 'Empty.'"

As he drives in circles: "Trust me, I know a really great fishing hole around here."

"Sure I'd let you borrow one of my favorite lures, only I didn't bring them today."

10 Clues That Your Car Isn't the Right Tow Vehicle for Your New Boat

1. The boat you wish to tow has a larger engine than your car.

2. The boat you wish to tow can sleep more people comfortably than you can squeeze sitting upright into your car.

3. Each time you try to tow your boat uphill, you find yourself going back downhill, with the boat as the new lead vehicle.

4. When you stomped on the gas to move your determinedly parked boat, the hitch tore off your car but the boat remained stationary.

5. Your car's owner's manual doesn't contain any information at all on towing or towing specifications.

6. The mechanics at your car dealership laughed uproariously when you told them you were going to trailer your new boat, and started making lists of what they were going to buy with their anticipated bonuses.

7. When the car and the boat trailer are attached, the boat completely covers the car in its shade.

8. When the car and the boat trailer are attached, your car's front wheels are off the ground.

9. You could park two of your car inside your boat.

10. Your car was parked near your boat when the boat's name was painted on and the painters stenciled the word "Dinghy" on its rear bumper.

Books That Aren't in the Bass Pro Shop's Catalog

Emergency Repairs at Sea, by **Orya Sink**

Winterizing Your Boat, by **Lotta Work**

Modern Fishing Techniques, by **Skunk Tagin**

The History of Cigarette, by **Awl Power**

*Things You Need to Know About Your
Boat Insurance Coverage,* by **Justine Kase**

Basic Lobster Hunting, by **Happy Crabbe**

How to Maintain a Boat on $1 a Year,
by **Howard I. Know**

It Was the Best of Times, It Was the Worst of Times…,
by **Nubo Towner**

Be Your Own Boat Mechanic, by **Axl Greece**

Twenty Miles from Shore and No Beer Left,
by **Willy Makit**

Lost at Sea, by **Flo Tinalong**

The Malfunctioning Gas Gauge and
Other Little Annoyances, by **Ron Onfumes**

Wooden Boat Plans, by **Bill Jerome Bhote**

How to Sell a Boat in a Weekend, by **H. Houdini**

I Was Shark Bait!, by **Walter Skier**

29 Handy Excuses to Get out of Work When You'd Rather Be Fishing

(Warning: Use with discretion, and don't kill off more grandparents than you actually have. People tend to catch on.)

1. I have the flu.

2. I have a toothache.

3. My kid/wife/dog has a toothache.

4. My little toe is stuck in the shower drain.

5. I'm allergic to the mold that's accumulated in the office air-conditioning system.

6. I've scheduled appointments out of the office today. (If someone should ask who your appointment is with, garble your response. Unless of course your fishing partner is the "business associate" you are supposedly going to see.)

7. I sprained my back/neck/shoulder/wrist/knee/ankle.

8. My cat is about to have kittens.

9. My horoscope says I should stay home.

10. My doctor says I should stay off my feet. (If they ask you why, pretend there's static on the line and that you can't hear them, and then quickly hang up.)

11. I broke my glasses/misplaced my contact lenses and can't see.

12. I've got the (name the disease of your choice) and I'm contagious.

13. It's Friday the 13th.

14. My car won't start.

15. My gerbil just died.

16. My grandmother is missing in the Bermuda Triangle and I really should stay home by the phone in case there's any news.

17. My psychiatrist says I need some time alone

18. My driver's license expired.

19. A UFO just landed in my backyard.

20. I'm clinically depressed over news of the declining shark population.

21. I have an earache.

22. I have a severe sinus infection.

23. I have a parole hearing.

24. My mother and father are finally getting married today.

25. My feet have a malodorous fungus.

26. I have an appointment for a urinalysis.

27. My dentures needed an extralong soaking.

28. My grandmother/grandfather/natural mother/ natural father/stepmother/stepfather/second step-mother/second stepfather/aunt/uncle/cousin/ neighbor just died.

29. I've just died

The 10 Worst Habits of Quirky Fishing Partners

1. He owns a miniaturized ruler that he photographs next to his minuscule catches to make his 5-inch fish appear 12 inches long, and he won't let you use it.

2. When he does finally scream, "I've got one," you know that chances are his lure is caught on your lure again.

3. One out of ten of his back casts ends up with him snagging you.

4. He can repeat word-for-word entire scenes from Arnold Schwarzenegger movies, and does so repeatedly and with gusto.

5. He likes to make animal sounds, which he believes attracts the larger fish.

6. He constantly complains about the lack of a women in his life. (You can smile silently at this, secure in the knowledge that soon he'll be

griping about the lack of a fishing partner, when you get back to shore and dump him.)

7. In an attempt to attract women to his smelly, belching self, he has taken up reading books with meaningful plots. And when the fish aren't biting he wants to discuss those books with you.

8. He thinks of himself as a "Stud Angler."

9. He thinks of your tackle box as his.

10. He takes small bites out of the bait when he thinks you're not looking. (Even when he's using the Roadkill Bait System.)

The Fisherman's Guide to Dressing for Success

What You Wear:	What It Says (Or Doesn't Say) About You:
Camo fatigues	"I am a rugged fisherman, and may use dynamite when you're not looking."
A moth-eaten fishing tournament hat from a tournament that hasn't been in existence since the late '70s	Let me tell you about the best day of my life.. the day I won the _____ tournament."
Perfectly coordinated Columbia fishing attire	"I've never caught a bloody fish."

What You Wear:	What It Says (Or Doesn't Say) About You:
A Grateful Dead T-shirt, cutoffs, and non–marine soled sandals	"Because I am the only one who can operate the ultracomplex fish finder and navigation software, I expect you to deify me."
A T-shirt with the slogan "Fish or Die"	"It's not my own death I'm talking about."
For the otherwise rational female: A bikini on a cold, overcast day	"My boyfriend says that I can pose with his next fish and maybe get my picture in a sporting magazine."

10 Clues That You May Not Get as Much out of a Fishing Seminar as You Originally Planned

1. The seminar is being held at a roadside rest stop.

2. The rain location is a Chuck E. Cheese's.

3. Most of the speakers at one time or other have accidentally broken off the tip of their rod by slamming it in a truck door.

4. These are the rods they are using to demonstrate their techniques.

5. The three speakers you went to listen to are mysteriously absent. Later you learn that they're all in the hospital after being involved in a major back-casting accident during rehearsal.

6. The man who caused the above accident chooses you out of the two hundred people in attendance to help him demonstrate his questionable technique.

7. The seminar's only sponsor can't be there because he's been arrested for fraudulent advertising practices and overall product misrepresentation.

8. All the door prizes are in once-opened boxes that have been resealed with duct tape.

9. Before the seminar begins, the head speaker gives out an address for attendees to report missing parts from their door prizes to.

10. Like your spirits, the clouds above you soon darken, and you find yourself forced to move to the rain location, only to discover that you are now sharing space with a hunting seminar, and have arrived just in time for the target practice segment of their program.

Arkansas Fishing Facts

1. Using a shop vac to land a fish has just been deemed illegal in all official Arkansas state tournaments (where there are witnesses).

2. Meanwhile, the rousing debate regarding the use of a 12-gauge shotgun during state-sanctioned events continues.

3. The largest growth spurt for an Arkansas bass occurs between the time he is hauled aboard an angler's boat and the time the angler first talks about the "monstrous" fish he caught.

4. Less than 1 percent of all Arkansas fishermen end up working for the FBI, because most can't pass a polygraph test.

5. Arkansas women who spray on fish oil instead of perfume are 72 percent more likely to "reel in" a husband than those who don't.

6. While which lure works best in Arkansas waters is still under heated debate, a cool beer was unanimously voted the top lure to attract

an Arkansas fisherman. (A fact of which the remaining 28 percent of non-fish-oiled Arkansas women are well aware!)

7. The Leaning Tower of Pisa once housed a tackle shop owned by Arkansas's Bubba "Skunked Again" Johnson, who insisted on keeping nearly a million sinkers all on the same side of the store.

8. Casting techniques have gotten so bad in Arkansas that the state is considering sanctioning a tree-bass tournament league.

9. Arkansas boasts the dubious honor of appearing in *Sightings* only fishing-related story—"I was abducted by an alien bass!"

10. After winning the state beer chug-a-lug contest for the tenth year in a row, state Senator Spanky "Not to Be Confused with Ted" Kennedy recently pushed through a ruling prohibiting Elvis impersonators from entering bass tournaments.

10 Clues That You're at a Bad Marina

1. All the trees and sea life are dead, but just about every other object is alive and glowing an eerie green.

2. The marina manager has a framed photo of Norman Bates in his office.

3. The expiration dates on the food in the marina store go back to the 1920s.

4. Happy hour is from 7 A.M. to 7 P.M.

5. The waters around your boat are serving as a mutant frog experiment for the local high school.

6. They're filming *Friday the 13th Part MCMXII* in the slip next to yours.

7. All the other boat owners seem to get very hairy during a full moon.

8. The maintenance men are Yogi and Bobo.

9. The marinas porta-potties were the source of inspiration for several *X-Files* episodes.

10. The boat slip you're assigned is surrounded by yellow "Crime Scene—Do Not Cross" tape.

10 Clues That Fishing and Boating Have Taken over Your Brain

1. The only time you're away from your boat for more than five consecutive days is during the Fort Lauderdale Boat Show, when you're frantically purchasing new gear for said boat.

2. You started a petition to make the first day of the Dania Marine Flea Market an official holiday so that you can get off from work and be there to get the best buys when it opens.

3. You drive your wife crazy because you remember everything about the day you bought the boat, but regularly forget your wedding anniversary (including the year in which the vows were said).

4 Your five-year-old house is literally falling down from neglect, but your boat looks as good as the day you bought her twelve years ago.

5. You named your dog after the manufacturer of your precious boat.

6. You named the family cat Johnson, after your outboard. (The alternate name was Bilge Buddy, which your family quickly vetoed.)

7. You never make an airline flight without bringing along the emergency ditch kit from your boat—including but not limited to: an inflatable life vest, waterproof flares, a water-proof handheld VHF, signal mirror, emergency water and rations—as carry-on luggage.

8. You bring an air horn to your son's little league games to cheer him on. (Or you did, until last week's run-in with that angry mother's group.)

9. When your daughter said that she needed a new pen for school, you mistakenly took her to the nearest tackle shop and bought her a Penn 9500 spinning reel.

10. Last Valentine's Day you got your boat $100 worth of Zyrex High Performance Bottom Coating, while your wife got a card.

5 Things Best Left at Home During a Fishing Trip

🐟 Witnesses.

🐟 Any gadget that seemed like a good idea when you saw it on sale next to the tackle shop cash register as you waited for the shop owner to dole out your live bait.

🐟 A camera. (1) If you don't catch a big fish, but want to fraudulently claim that you did, it's best to be able to honestly state right up front that you had no camera on board and therefore they're going to just have to take you at your word. (2) If you actually do catch a large fish that you'd like to be photographed with, chances are your camera will have been knocked overboard in the struggle to land your seafaring monster and your film is now waterlogged and completely useless.

🐟 A certified scale, for the same reasons as (1) above.

Your boat-towing membership card. You know deep in your heart that the only person who will come out to get you in his rickety tow boat will have never heard of the company who issued the card.

The Perfect Fishing Vest

When properly loaded, the perfect fishing vest should weigh at least thirty pounds. The following is a list of gear that every self-respecting angler needs to keep attached to himself at all times:

1. 100 assorted sinkers, distributed evenly throughout your vest for obvious reasons.

2. 278 assorted hooks needing sharpening.

3. A hook sharpener.

4. A line cutter.

5. A box of 100 Band-Aids for when you injure yourself using the line cutter.

6. Every multi-plier on the market.

7. Enough Snickers bars that they've given you complimentary stock in the company.

8. A water-resistant camera to prove to your friend that for once (heavy emphasis on the *once*), you're telling the truth.

9. 30 rolls of 36-exposure film to make sure you don't miss a shot (or you wouldn't have if you hadn't forgotten to buy new camera batteries).

10. A copy of this book to pass the time when the fish aren't biting.

11. A second joke book because they haven't been biting at all lately.

12. A comprehensive compact first-aid kit that includes a mini do-it-yourself surgical kit. (Your wife made you bring this along, but now that you think back on your last few fishing expeditions...you stuff it into your pocket when no one is looking.)

13. Someone else's ID, for unexpected encounters with the game warden.

And because you just never know what adversity you might encounter:

14 A spare VHF radio.

15. Extra fully charged cellular phone batteries.

16. Signal flares large enough to alert the entire state that you're in trouble.

17. A comprehensive West System fiberglass repair kit.

18. A Datrex emergency fishing kit: In case the hole in your boat is larger than the amount of epoxy in your emergency repair kit, and all the

fishing equipment that you mortgaged your house to buy goes down with your boat, which drowns your spare flares and electronics in the process, leaving you stranded.

19. A book of risqué jokes to revive your spirits after losing the above-mentioned gear.

20. A pint of your own blood, which your wife will want when she finds out that you've lost the above-mentioned gear and boat.

Why Dogs Make Better Fishing Buddies Than Humans Do

1. Dogs are loyal, faithful, and don't lie about how they've caught bigger fish than you.

2. Dogs don't steal your favorite lures (though an especially cute puppy might steal your heart).

3. Once back at the dock, a dog won't tell tales about what a bad day on the water you had.

4. Dogs will listen to endless repetitions of your "big one" story without complaint.

5. A dog will never arrive at your boat attired in perfectly color-coordinated pastel fishing clothes that just scream out...geek.

6. A dog will never drink the last beer. (The same, however, cannot be said of the last turkey sandwich in the cooler.)

7. A dog will never try to guess how much you paid for your boat and then snidely tell you that you should have gone to his Uncle Bubba for a better deal.

8. Dogs rarely call at the last minute to say they're sick (especially if there's going to be the above-mentioned cooler packed with sandwiches on board).

9. Dogs don't demand a turn driving your brand-new, ostentatiously overpowered fishing machine.

10. A dog will never tell that you were napping when the big one that you'd waited for your entire life arrived, nibbled at your bait, and, with a good-bye splash, left for better waters (because he will have been napping right alongside you).

The Truth About Fishing Seminars

1. The most useful fishing tips are often found in the brochure advertising the seminar rather than at the seminar itself.

2. Frequently, the person who learns the most at a fishing seminar is the person giving the seminar.

3. It's easy to spot a fishing-seminar addict—he's the one wearing his collection of name badges with all the pride of a four-star general wearing his military commendations.

4. Beginner fishing-seminars are the sport fishing industry's version of "Barney."

5. Fishing seminars are a great way to meet new friends who:
    (a) you have much in common with,
    (b) haven't yet heard your often-told fishing tales,
    (c) own a boat and will take you out fishing until your wife lets you buy your own boat.

6. Another way to spot a fishing-seminar addict: He's the one who has a "Hello, my name is _____" burned in on his favorite shirt, though the actual stickers have long since been removed.

7. "I don't really know any more about fishing than I did when I walked in the door, but now my ignorance has been organized." (Seminar attendee)

8. Another surefire way to spot a fishing-seminar addict: He's the one who takes twelve hours' worth of notes during a six-hour seminar.

9. Nick "Skunked Again" Parsons holds the world record for fishing-seminar attendance, having attended 945 seminars and 560 miniseminars in the past twenty years. And he has the notes and the hemorrhoids, if not the catches, to prove it.

10. Now, if you'll just take a minute and fill out our twelve-page seminar evaluation form...

You Know You've Been out Fishing Unsuccessfully in the Hot Sun for Way Too Long, When You...

Start thinking of ways to mount your remaining live bait on the walls of your den.

Take pictures of yourself holding up your live bait proudly.

Decide to practice casting with your other hand.

Begin to miss your spouse.

Hum "My Way" as you cast.

Put two lures on the end of your line to increase your chances of catching something.

Talk to yourself, answer, get into a fight,
and lose that fight.

Polish your lures.

Reorganize your tackle box for the
twelfth time today.

Pull out your ear hairs.

Run out of ear hairs to remove.

Start telling yourself your favorite fish stories,
and "ooh" and "aah" at the appropriate times.

Think about having another child.

Can't recall how many children, if any,
you already have.

Drive your boat in tight figure eights
at top speed.

Make a detailed list of the most discrete fish
markets for you to shop at on the way home.

10 Clues That Taking Your Teenage Nephew Fishing Isn't as Good an Idea as You Originally Thought

1. He arrives wearing sneakers that cost more than your boat.

2. You hand him a fishing rod and he asks what it is.

3. You hand him a hook and he pushes it through his nose and exclaims, "Wait till the kids at school see this!"

4. After you get the hook out of his nose and give him the necessary first aid, you hand him an Uncle Josh Pork Rind to put on the hook and instead he eats it and asks for another one.

5. Fifteen minutes away from the dock and he's drunk all your beer.

6. As he loosens up, he begins to talk expertly about the use of plastic explosives as an alternative to conventional lures.

7. As a gesture of friendship, he shows you his parole officer's photo, which he keeps in his wallet.

8. He repeatedly asks, "When does the fun start?"

9. When you finally get a Big One on the line, he leans out too far to check out the babes in a nearby speed boat and falls overboard so that you're forced to let your fish go as you dive in to rescue him.

10. He thinks you're kidding as you begin to make plans to use him as chum.

More Things Best Left at Home During a Fishing Trip

A book of 1,001 fishing disaster jokes

A copy of *Women Who Love Men Who Only Love to Fish*

Free advice

A bucket. Chances are it's only going to end up being worn on someone's foot.

Any in-laws, no matter how many times they try to sneak on board, or what they offer to pay for

More than two spare rolls of duct tape; after using up two rolls you're probably going to have to put on your life jacket and swim for it anyway

A copy of *Women Who Love Men Who Only Love Women Who Hold IGFA Records*

Things You Do Want to Bring on Your Next Fishing Trip

🎣 A camera filled with previously taken photos of you with large fish. (Note: Be sure not to get the fish market and other identifying give-aways in the photos.)

🎣 A can of salmon for lunch. That way you can honestly say that you saw some fish on your outing.

🎣 A professional fishing guide.

🎣 Dynamite—to ensure a significant catch when the authorities aren't looking.

🎣 A lucky rabbit's foot. In a pinch, the fur can be used to make a halfway decent fly.

Lots and lots of sinkers. These are best utilized on your fishing buddy who just caught that state-record fish, with no other witness than you.

A spoon lure. If the fish aren't interested, you can use it to pry open a stuck push tab on a beer can.

If you're going out on a fishing party boat, wear your Jason from *Friday the 13th* costume from last Halloween and your fellow anglers are guaranteed to let you use any rod you choose...or all of them if you like.

7 Places You Don't Want to Fish

1. Chernobyl.

2. Uncle Bubba's favorite fishing hole. (Uncle Bubba's got a pretty mean elephant gun.)

3. In the lake directly in front of the game warden's office.

4. Anyplace where the water glows at night.

5. Anyplace where the water is glowing at night because of the bioluminescent little green men bathing in it.

6. Anyplace where the remaining fish from the waters with the little green men can now be found on *Unsolved Mysteries* searching for their lost finned friends.

7. New York City.

10 Clues That You Need a New Fishing Partner

1. He's a fan of both *The Oprah Winfrey Show* and *Sally Jessy Raphael*.

2. Or worse, he's appeared on both *The Oprah Winfrey Show* and *Sally Jessy Raphael*.

3 When you run out of beer, he drinks from the baitwell.

4. Or worse, he drinks Zima instead of beer.

5. He insists on bringing a camp stove on board so that he can make Kraft Macaroni & Cheese for lunch, just like his mom cooks for him when she's not in jail.

6. Or worse, he insists that you both eat cucumber finger sandwiches.

7. He forgot to set his VCR for *Cops* and had to detour home to do so.

8. Or worse, he explains that he's late because of a little misunderstanding with a SWAT team.

9. He can't stay out after dark because of his parole restrictions.

10. Or worse, he firmly refuses to stay out late fishing on a Saturday, because he doesn't want to miss a moment of *Dr. Quinn, Medicine Woman.*

The Facts About Fishing-
Tournament Board Meetings

1. The amount of work decisions made at a tournament board meeting is normally in direct *dis*proportion to the number of people attending said meeting.

2. The ease with which a board member can get his or her point across during a morning meeting is in direct proportion to the amount of donuts at the meeting.

3. Scheduling meetings when many of the intended participants are unable to attend will considerably reduce opposition to your ideas.

4. The ability to talk without pause for two straight hours will further reduce any opposition toward your proposed plans (by inducing catatonia instead).

5. To further increase the odds in your favor, hold a separate meeting with each board member concerned. This allows you to present the results of those individual meetings to others with your own slant (i.e., if there were no witnesses, and you're brave enough, you can stretch the truth quite a bit about what was said).

6. Casually mentioning to a fellow board member that you'll be helping them get their proposal passed at the next meeting should help guarantee their vote.

7. To avoid boredom at meetings, bring along your cellular phone and discretely dial the other board members' cellular phone and/or beeper numbers when they start to get too long-winded.

14 Things to Do to Drive Your Wife Absolutely Crazy So That She'll *Insist* That You Get out of the House and Go Fishing

1. Call her by the dog's name and then deny it.

2. Answer all her questions with a question, preferably one on a totally different subject.

3. Krazy Glue the commode seat in the men's up position.

4. Shrink her jeans and when she overreacts, say that you prefer her with some meat on her bones.

5. Firmly refuse to ever ask for directions even if you find yourself in Georgia waters when your original destination was California.

6. Call her by your mother's name and then deny it.

7. Start a conversation with the dog in the middle of one with her.

8. Buy her power tools for Valentine's Day.

9. Never give her a straight answer.

10. Take up yodeling and practice a lot.

11. Quote Tim Allen to validate your position during arguments. (Argh! Argh! Argh!)

12. Leave the newspaper open to an ad for plastic surgery.

13. Pretend you forgot how to speak English.

14. Answer every question with "Yes, dear." (Use with caution as PMS is a valid murder defense in most states.)

14 Uses for a Dead Fishing Buddy

1. Official "witness" to your biggest catch ever

2. Bait

3. Dock fender

4. Replacement trailer bunk

5. Rod holder

6. Rod rack

7. Fish bat

8. Bobber

9. Good luck charm

10. Trophy

11. Kite rod

12. Paddle

13. Outboard motor bracket

14. Lightning rod

10 Great Reasons to Fish

(That Are for the Most Part Acceptable to the General Public)

1. It gets you out on the water, where a boat filled with babes in bikinis may occasionally pass by.

2. It builds manly self-esteem in a way that playing tennis and *Jeopardy!* don't.

3. The overwhelmingly primitive satisfaction that comes with periodically besting one's prey, tossing it on the grill, and inviting everyone you've ever met over to eat it. (Try that with a tennis ball!)

4. What's a weekend without at least one hook stuck in your thumb?

5. It's a chance to get away from the pressures of everyday life and recurring thoughts of your desk-jockey boss who won't give you the promotion you so richly deserve. (Your next meeting with him may be a good opportunity to break in your new fish bat.)

6. It's an excuse to wear manly fishing gear.

7. If one does occasionally drink too much, it's much more macho to "chum" over the side rather than to just be a Saturday afternoon lush heaving in one's own backyard.

8. You must use all three hundred lures you bought on sale last year because your wife said at the time of purchase that she'd take a chain saw to you if you didn't.

9. If you practice enough, you can show off at the upcoming casting clinic at the next boat show.

10. Going fishing is much better than working around the house, attending family weddings and funerals, spending time with visiting out-of-town relatives, or working overtime on weekends. The possibilities for using fishing to avoid life are only limited by your imagination and any foolish need you may have to tell the truth!

"Stop Drinking the Water out of the Baitwell!" And Other Extremely Irritating Habits of Fellow Fishermen

The Borrower:

He uses your rods, reels, and tackle, drinks your beer, and never offers to chip in for gas. The only thing he brings to a day of fishing is his camera, so that he can pose with your fish.

The Pig Pen:

You can accurately follow his path around your boat by his trail of beer rings and greasy potato chips.

Mr. Obnoxious: He's family visiting from out of town, which is the only reason you allowed yourself to be conned into allowing him near your precious boat. He tries the patience of a saint and holds the dubious honor of being the only person ever slugged by the pope.

Mr. Flatulent: His bodily functions are so loud that there aren't any fish brave enough to come within a mile of your boat.

The Speed Demon: You've just found the perfect quiet fishing spot, one where the fish are doing everything but jumping into your boat to help you catch them, when he comes zooming up at full tilt, well above the local speed limit, to "see how you're doing."

Speed Demon with a Badge: At this point you're so frustrated at the sight of the large fish that are quickly scattering away from your boat after his noisy arrival that you'd call the local game warden to complain, only the guy in the other boat is the local game warden.

15 Handy Excuses for When You Get Caught Speeding

1. My passengers made me do it—ticket them.

2. I just sped to get your attention, Officer. By the way, do you have any plans for tonight?

3. This wasn't a No Wake Zone last week, honest.

4. Take pity on me, I'm just learning how to drive a boat. I thought you would have guessed that because there's a Club Nautico decal on the side.

5. The guy in the Fountain was going twice as fast as I was.

6. We needed to get more ice before the beer gets warm.

7. My speedometer must be malfunctioning. (Hit it repeatedly for good effect.)

8. I had to speed or the Hustler behind me would have creamed me. Hey, where did he go?

9. I'm having chest pains and I was rushing back to the dock for medical attention. Want to give me a marine patrol escort?

10. I have to get to the gas dock, I'm nearly out of gas.

11. How was I supposed to know what the speed limit was? It isn't posted.

12. The throttle got jammed.

13. The water was so flat and the weather so pleasant that I really had no idea I was doing fifty in a No Wake Zone.

When fishing in south Florida, you can try:

14. Don Johnson drove like this in *Miami Vice*. I thought it was the way you all drove down here.

But don't ever use:

15. I just stole this boat and I'm still learning the controls.

Things You Never Want to Hear from Your Fishing Charter Captain

"Sorry, our insurance doesn't cover rods lost overboard."

"That's by far the nicest hubcap we've ever hauled aboard."

"I've never seen a bug bite get this big so fast."

"Oh no, how do I explain this?"

"Hey, Bubba, get this, he thinks that lunch is included in the price of his fishing trip."

"That was the policy of the guy who used to own this fishing outfit, not us."

"By the way, do you have any experience with underwater fiberglass repair?"

"The verification machine won't accept
your credit card."

"In my twenty-nine years of fishing these
waters, I've never seen a reel get this tangled."

"Grab a bucket and start bailing."

"I'm going to have to throw all nonessential
items—such as your tackle box—overboard."

"We haven't seen those fish in these waters
in years. Is that what you traveled all
this way for?"

"Looks like this storm is going to
get particularly nasty."

"The life jackets are in the storage hatch
next to the livewell."

"Do you believe in miracles?"

And back at the dock:

"Bet you thought we weren't going to make it."

"Tipping is appreciated."

"Did I mention that I'm also the sheriff?"

20 Viable Substitutes for Traditional Bait and Lures

- Those obnoxious blinking lights in the soles of kids' sneakers

- Last years' ASPCA tag from your dog

- Your wife's silver dangling earrings

- Your mother-in-law (cut up in small chunks for jigging or thin strips for trolling)

- A 1949 DeSoto hubcap

- The hood ornament from your pretentious boss's Mercedes

- Rubber Mickey Mouse finger puppets

- Minnie Mouse puppets, too

- The cat that keeps digging up your backyard (see usage info re: "mother-in-law")

- Key-chain flashlights

- Roadkill

- Sterling silver napkin rings

- Bottle corks

- Small Milk-Bones

- The CD of the Month Club main selection (cut down to appropriate size)

- Velveeta (same as roadkill)

- The kid next door who's just taken up the drums

- Last week's "mystery meat"

- Almost all small office supplies (much to your employer's delight)

- For female anglers: Your boyfriend's little black book will increase your catches while decreasing his.

"The Dog Ate My Prize Catch" and Other Pet Alibis

- I missed the tournament start because the dog buried my alarm clock in the backyard.

- The dog knocked my morning coffee over on the flies that I'd worked all night to tie, so I'm going to have to borrow some of yours.

- I missed the tournament start because my German shepherd banged into my open truck door, shutting it, and locking my boat keys inside.

- No, I wasn't trying to avoid living up to my promise to take you fishing, the dog knocked my phone receiver off the hook.

- I must have been out walking the dog when you called.

You left messages? Really? Well, the dog chewed on the phone line going to the answering machine and it hasn't taken messages right since.

That's so kind of you to offer to bring the beer, but I'm not taking the boat out tomorrow, you see, my mini dachshund's puppies are due any minute.

I can't go fishing with you today, the dog ate my dentures.

15 Excuses for Being Late for the Weigh-In

1. The engine broke down a couple of times.

2. No one told us what time the weigh-in was.

3. We couldn't get to the dock in time, there were too many other boats in our way. Who's organizing this thing, anyway?

4. We're not the only boat that's late.

5. We stopped to rescue the crew of a sinking boat. (You'd better have some wet people on board—genuine rescues or not—if you expect the tournament officials to believe this one.)

6. We caught so many fish that it slowed our return speed considerably.

7. The captain's glasses fell overboard and our return trip was touch-and-go.

8. Our angler hurt his back and we had to take things slow and easy.

9. We stopped to assist the local marine patrol. Sorry, I didn't get the officer's name.

10. We called ahead on our cellular phone.

11. My watch says we're on time. (Note: Don't forget to adjust your watch before making this statement.)

12. The man over there said everything was okay. Hey, where'd he go?

13. The sun was in my eyes the entire way back; it made driving the boat difficult.

14. Daylight savings time has ended? I didn't know that. That explains the problem.

15. No, I would never lie to you.

Reminiscing About the Day's Catch

To the fishing partner and only witness:

"I think we did right fine today, don't you?" On days when the catch is extremely minimal, the subject should be quickly changed before your partner can respond.

To the skeptical wife who cooks your catch:

"There's more there than at first glance. Definitely enough for a small meal." Or: "Twenty years ago they grew a *lot* bigger."

To the young son:

"One of these days I'm going to take you with me and show you what being a man is all about."

To the young daughter:

"Are you watching *Pocahantas* AGAIN?!"

To the male neighbors (after making sure they didn't see you sneak your small catch into the house):

"I take a primitive satisfaction in being able to go out with a rod and reel and a few old lures and come back with enough to feed my family. It makes me want to beat my chest and yell like a proud caveman."

To the coworkers who have suffered through years of your unverified catch reports:

"I would have had the most impressive photos if the camera hadn't been dropped and then leaked light, which exposed the entire roll."

To the know-it-all father-in-law, a fellow fisherman who always does better than you when you go out together:

"We finally had to let the monster go. It was either that or risk sinking the boat when we brought it aboard."

During the nightly fisherman's prayer:

"Please, God, let me catch a real fish tomorrow."

How to Tell if Your Kid Is a Junior Fishaholic

1. He does his school book reports on: *Hook, Line & Sinker: A Complete Guide to Terminal Tackle*, *The Fishing Hall of Shame*, and *The Bass Bible*.

2. He dressed up as Mark Sosin for Halloween (and scared the entire neighborhood).

3. As a baby, he preferred teething on a Moldcraft plastic chugger (unrigged, of course) rather than a pacifier.

4. When he discovered girls, he tried using a 9/0 hook to "catch" one.

5. His school science-fair project was entitled "How to Taxidermy Your Fish at Home."

6. He put his science-fair award on the shelf next to his fillet knife collection.

7. His subscription to *Angler* doesn't run out until 2049.

8. Instead of baseball cards, he collects multipliers and other rigging tools.

9. He ended up in detention because he used his fists to defend his right to wear his favorite T-shirt, which reads: "Knot Tying Tools Are for Sissies."

10. He'll only go to college when they come up with a major in "Fish Population Control."

Potential Fishing Buddies to Avoid

Choosing the right fishing buddy is more important than choosing your first through third wives, your career path (a.k.a. dead-end job) and in many cases, even more important than the selection of your fishing boat (which, if possible, is heavily overpowered to help you get to the good spots first). The following guidelines should take some of the stress out of this complex decision-making process, and help you know what to avoid:

Mr. I Can Fish BetterThan You Can	He's arrogant, he's irritating, and worst of all, on some days he's right.
Mr. I Bet I Can Fish Better Than You Do Today	Same as above, only he's so sure of himself that he wants to take your money in what he views as a "sucker bet."

The Ruthless Sportsman

He's going to catch a fish no matter how long it takes. And will rouse you from that nap you snuck during the day trip that turned into an all-nighter with a shouted, "Wake up, you weenie!"

The Fishing Stud

Uses enough hair spray to fish through a hurricane without one hair getting out of place. He constantly says that the right bait for him is a boat full of scantily clad women and should one ever stop by...you'd be only too glad to help him aboard it.

Mr. Perpetual Optimist

So constantly cheerful, even on days when the only fish biting are in another county, that one day you know that the stress is going to get to you and you're going to burst a blood vessel and cut him up for bait.

Mr. Sensitive

Doesn't actually want to catch the fish as it might "hurt them." You don't have to wait until the pressure gets to you—use him for bait NOW!

The Psuedo-Sportsman

He wears all the right clothes, owns all the right gear…and it ends right there. He possesses no fishing skills whatsoever. In his opinion that's what you're for. Note: This relationship can work if he owns an expensive boat that you've lusted over but can't afford, and he will pay for your gear, buys beer, and doesn't take it personally if you leave him at the dock.

The Ex-Con

Warning: One should not consider a fishing partner who has more than two felony convictions, no matter what his skills on the water.

Just Got out of the State Hospital

One step above the ex-con, he was smart enough to fake insanity and get sentenced to cushier surroundings. At least you hope he was faking…

The Cola Junkie

"What do you mean we don't have any sugar and caffeine left on board!" His hands shake too much to reel in a decent-size fish.

The Neighbors' Ten-Year-Old Kid

You may be tempted to tell yourself that since he's young, you can mold him to your ways. Don't share this naive thought with him. You'll only get a lot of laughter and receive a clipped, "Yeah, right" before he returns his fixated attention to his handheld electronic game.

The Ozzy Osborne Fan

I'm sure you know what he likes to do with the live fish.

LASTLY, NEVER, EVER consider a fishing buddy who has been on *America's Most Wanted, Unsolved Mysteries,* or any show featuring people talking about their UFO experiences.

The Fishing Captain Revealed

To help the average beleaguered fishing crew better understand the eccentric psyche of their screaming captain, it should be noted that the average fishing boat captain will fall into one of the eight standard categories:

The Cheerleader...   "Okay guys, we're out here to win! win! win!"

The Traditionalist...   "Let me make one thing clear: We either win today or I'll be using you as chum tomorrow."

The Techno-Brat...   "Of course, we're going to win today. In addition to the most high-tech fishing gear that my father's money can buy, I've just installed a computer system that provides updated four-color satellite charts every fifteen minutes showing concise water temperatures and currents so that we can best guesstimate the most productive fishing spots."

The Realist... "In addition to all our high tech fishing gear, I've taken the liberty of bringing along a healthy supply of dynamite "

Mr. By-the-Book... "Look, right here on page forty seven of *The Orvis Guide* it says..."

The Do-It-Myselfer... "Today I'll be driving the boat to my favorite fishing holes, choosing the lures we will be using, and offering other help ful tips as the day goes on ″

The Director... "Now I want you all to have your rods at hand from the moment we leave the dock. I want us to all look alert and ready, like the skilled fishing team that we are. Tony, I want you to stand stage left, while Marty you'll..."

And then there's every crew's favorite...
The Absentee Captain.
It must be noted at this point that some captains will fall into more than one category during a day of

fishing, depending upon several factors, the most influential of which is the size of the fish that's just taken the bait.

SECOND NOTE: A crew mutiny that results in throwing the captain overboard does not reclassify him as an Absentee Captain. In most states a seven-year wait is required.

How to Spot a Techno-Fisherman

1. His helm resembles the cockpit of the Concorde.

2. He has a satellite TV mini-dish on his radar arch.

3. While waiting for a fish to bite, he sits on deck and sends E-mail to his Internet buddies via a cell phone connection to his laptop PC.

4. He has a weather fax set up on deck next to his livewell so that he can get the latest info on surface conditions and water temperature while fishing.

5. Like an airplane pilot, he has three of each instrument on board; that way, if one malfunctions, he can tell which one it is.

6. He uses only Kool Mate Electric Igloos because he firmly believes that "ice should be in one's drink, not on the outside of it keeping it cold." Even his dead bait and caught fish are kept in an electric cooler.

7. He wears a Tide Watch to bed.

The Fishing Bargain

Three anglers were fishing a tournament where no fish were biting.

"I can't believe this," the first angler complained. "Do you know that since today is my anniversary I had to promise my wife dinner at Martha's, where it's a minimum of fifty dollars a plate, just so I could go fishing today?"

"You think that's bad," the second angler broke in. "Today is my kid's birthday. In order to calm my wife down I had to agree to let her mother come visit us for a week."

When the third man, an elderly angler, didn't immediately jump in, the first two turned to stare at him. The third angler shrugged. "I just did what I always do. I whisper something kinky in my wife's ear, and she tells me to get out of the house and go find something productive to do."

Fishing with Kids

When planning a family fishing trip that involves young children, there are a few tried and true techniques that will help you keep your sanity:

1. Create a series of audiotapes beforehand in which you rant and rave the normal overused parental phrases, such as, "I said NO!," "Sit down and behave," and "No, you can't toss your sister overboard to see if she floats." Then, when your offspring become unruly, simply insert the appropriate tape into the boat stereo and save your vocal chords from the accrued damage that comes with continual shouting.

2. If your children are going through a particularly unmanageable stage, and you're lucky enough to be fishing off a large sportfisher with a cabin, make a videotape of yourself lecturing them about their anticipated transgressions. Then, when little Nickie ties little Laurie to the anchor chain because she tried to drown him

in the livewell, all you have to do is lock them both below with your Academy Award video of parental chiding set to automatic replay. (Note: Break out the champagne and savor the momentary quiet. You know it's not going to last.)

3. If the cabin option isn't available and the boat stereo isn't working, you can still encourage good behavior in your youngsters by filling their little minds, for several days before you leave the dock, with tales of grotesque sea monsters who eat disobedient kids.

Tall-Fish-Tale Survival Skills

You're not exactly sure how your wife conned you into taking your obnoxious, long-winded, and somewhat gaseous father-in-law out on your precious fishing boat, which you bought solely so that you could go offshore to get away from him during his visits, but since many of us have been there with various irritating relatives ourselves, we're going to share our accumulated advice...

- Pass around potato chips, pretzels, and other crunchy junk food and, with the help of your fishing buddies, drown him out with your synchronized crunching.

- Ask so many questions that the old geezer's head spins and he falls overboard. (This is your chance to gun the engine and RUN! Your wife will eventually talk to you again...that is, if you want her to.)

🎣 Keep interrupting him with your own stories of even more unbelievable catches, until he gives up.

🎣 Open a magazine on a completely unrelated sports subject and begin to read.

🎣 Sew his lips shut with Berkley FireLine.

🎣 Pawn him off on a fishing neighbor (preferably one that you don't like much) who's only heard his stories a hundred or so times.

Some Thoughts on Fishing Boat Morale

The first thing a fishing boat captain has to understand about shipboard morale, whether he is a professional captain or a family man out for a day's angling with his wife and kids, is that as the captain it is his job to keep his crew happy...whether they like it or not.

Ideally, a fishing crew should be comprised of carefully chosen, special people who can rise above the petty grievances that normally crop up after a group of mariners spends too much time together on a floating hull that seems to get smaller with each passing hour, and despite minor disagreements, continue to exhibit enthusiasm and camaraderie, supporting and assisting each other in all their endeavors. It's either that or the captain has to put something into the drinking water tank.

🎣 Playing music on a boat will often soothe an unruly crew. (Note: Turning off the music will often have the same effect.)

🎣 A smart captain will never forget to remind his crew that in order for them to be happy, ultimately he too has to be happy.

🎣 Every crew should remember that it takes less than a day for a smiling, cheerful crew to drive the average captain completely insane.

🎣 A great captain is one who knows how to inspire his crew to band together in a common effort. (Preferably, though, that cause is not a mutiny.)

For Fishwives Only:
7 Clues That You Are Married
to a Fanatic Fisherman

1. Your fisherman-husband promises to cut the grass "just as soon as fishing season ends." That was back in 1979, your grass is now seven feet tall and every Saturday morning your neighbors gather together to picket in front of your house. (Not that you can see them over the grass.)

2. When high seas prevent him from fishing, he:

    Takes out the chain saw to cut down all the trees in the backyard that interfere with his casting practice.

    Wears black, the color of mourning.

And on rainy days, he:

    Sits in front of the television, totally able to ignore the screaming two-year-old who wants to be watching *Pocahantas* for the millionth time, as he salivates over "Successful Offshore Bait Rigging" featuring George Poveromo, which he has seen over two million times. (He's on his eighth copy of this video.)

3. You sent him to Anglers Anonymous and they sent him back.

4. Your house has a dolphin mailbox out front, and billfish statues jumping across the lawn (last seen in 1982 when the grass passed the three-foot mark). Your living room walls are covered in the works of Gray's Marine Taxidermy (much of which he bought on sale and didn't actually catch).

5. He tried to sell the aforementioned *Pocahantas*-loving two-year-old to pay for a weeklong fishing jaunt in Costa Rica.

6. His idea of a family trip is a monthlong visit to the International Game Fish Association museum.

If you are still in doubt that your ex-husband is a Wholly Fixated Fisherman:

7. You left him three months ago and he still hasn't noticed.

Lindsey's Law of Flares

That flare which is shot up
Shall most assuredly come down
Upon or into the most combustible
Vessel, building, or object
Available within a 37.4-square mile radius.

10 Common Boating Terms Explained

Anchor

The only part of a boat that admits to being "dead weight."

Bimini

(1) A canvas top to protect a boater from sunburn and keep the deck area cool. (2) An island surrounded by waters that are deep enough to sink your boat in for insurance purposes. (See "Tongue of the Ocean.")

Chart

A helpful diagram showing the underwater topography and associated invisible dangers for an area just adjacent to, but never covering, the area you are in.

Emergency Rations

The three Snickers bars you forgot in the pocket of your foul-weather jacket when you left it on board after the last time it rained, seven months ago.

Outboard

An attachment to your boat hull that creates a second hole in the water for you to throw your money in.

River

A body of water in which the current is running strongly in the direction opposite the one you want to go.

Tongue of the Ocean

(1) A geographical wonder with some of the deepest waters on the planet and the associated variety of rare fish and sea life. (2) The Graveyard for the Overinsured.

Top Speed

The efficiency with which a repair shop clerk can run up your charge card. Often leading to a trip to "Bimini" (see above).

VHF

The CB of the waterways, where bizarre call signals called "handles" on land are exchanged for even stranger boat names.

Waterskiing

Trolling for sharks.

Things You Don't Want to Hear from Your Boat Surveyor

1. Wild laughter

2. "I'm impressed that you've kept her afloat all these years."

3. Anything that indicates that he knows you're lying about the vessel's maintenance history.

4. "I've never seen fiberglass delamination like this. Would you mind if I took a piece so that researchers can study it?"

5. "I seem to have run out of paper and I'm not done making my repair recommendations list."

6. "In your case I don't think the BUC book value would apply."

7. "No, I don't think a fresh coat of wax will make much difference with potential sales."

8. "Sure the boat can be restored to new...if you win the lottery or inherit a large amount of money in the near future."

9. "I see that you've done some very impressive emergency hull repairs with JB Cold Weld. Just how many submerged rocks have you hit over the years?"

10. "Do you have good insurance? If so, I'd advise you taking her out on one last voyage...with a Zodiac life raft on board."

Politically Correct Boating

The following is an updated and thoroughly revised list of nautical terms in keeping with the politically correct nature of the 1990s:

Deck fluff	Female crew
Sinking	Flotation challenged
Hard aground	Temporarily ashore
Taking in water	Irrigating
Cooler	Beer condominium
Sunbathing	Vitamin D absorption
Party boat	Recreational vessel
Heavy weather	Global warming

Compass	Navigational electronics
First-aid kit	Spare beer cooler
Man overboard	More beer for us
Lost at sea	Location impaired
Channel 16	HELP!!!

Lindsey's Second
Law of Flares

A flare that is shot up
At the request of an approaching rescue vessel
To determine the exact location
Of the vessel in need of rescue
Has a 46.2 percent chance of coming down
Directly upon the rescue vessel
Necessitating the rescue of that vessel also.

Everything I Know, I Learned from My Boat

Regular washings makes people happier
to be around you.

Always maintain a balance in life,
especially when mixing oil and fuel in a
two-stroke engine.

The surest way to get someone's instant and
complete attention is to malfunction.

10 Things You Don't Want to Hear from an Electrician Working on Your Boat

1. The words "jury-rigged."

2. "I'm afraid this type of repair isn't covered under the warranty."

3. "Do you smell something burning?"

4. "This job is going to take a bit more work than we thought when we quoted our estimate."

5. "I think I found the problem. It appears that the boat's last owner tried to use telephone wiring instead of standard electrical wiring."

6. "Do you have good insurance?"

7. "It's nothing to worry about. You just blew a fuse. That'll be fifty dollars."

8. "Next time one of your electronics acts up, just give it a good smack on the side like this. That'll be fifty dollars."

9. Immediately upon stepping on board, "That'll be fifty dollars."

10. "There's nothing wrong with your boat's electrical system. As far as the mysteriously flickering lights go, I'd call the producers of *Sightings* if I was you."

Habits You Don't Want in the Boater in the Slip Next to Yours

1. He has a plastic pink flamingo collection, which he proudly displays on his deck.

2. He collects stolen road signs, which he proudly sets out between the pink flamingos.

3. He is allergic to mosquito bites and covers his cabin (which happily you can't see) and deck area (which, unfortunately, you can see) with No-Pest Strips, which he then forgets to change.

4. He's installed a basketball hoop on the piling between your boats so that his grandson can "drop a few sinkers" when he stays with them. Of course, the boy misses often, and the ball instead lands on your electronics and other on-deck valuables.

5. He has sensitive feet so he carpets his deck in a green and yellow shag rug remnant that after a heavy rain turns into a man-made lake, then a mold experiment worthy of Dr. Petri.

6. His idea of deck furniture consists of a weathered telephone cable spool as a table and cinder blocks as seats.

7. He calls his rusted-out hibachi an antique, and, if you let him, will chew your ear off with tales of the happy barbecues it's provided over the years.

8. All the plants on his boat are dead, but he won't throw them out because he believes that "all they need is some Miracle-Gro."

9. Since his wife won't let him keep his stuffed barracuda with the missing teeth in "her" living room...he's installed it proudly on "his" deck.

10. He sunbathes nude on deck when you have guests over.

11. And then there's your worst nightmare if he's a live-aboard boater...his wife finally gets as exasperated with him as you are and moves *him* permanently onto the deck.

Lindsey's Law of Mildew

It can be safely estimated
that, had Dr. Curie owned a boat,
she would have discovered penicillin
twenty-six years earlier.

10 Things You Don't Want to Hear from the Plumber Working on Your Boat

1. "You don't happen to have a five-gallon bucket, do you?"

2. "No, I'm not union. Though I do plan on joining the union just as soon as I pass the state certification test."

3. "No, that isn't the hourly rate, we charge in fifteen-minute increments."

4. The words "antique plumbing."

5. While unclogging the head: "I think I found what's left of your kid's turtle."

6. "This is some exotic galley you've got here, I've never seen fittings this size."

7. "Oops. I just broke off the rusty valve handle from the water tank."

8. As he cleans out a clogged shower drain: "I think I know where all the hair from the top of your head went."

9. "Unless you want me to install new plumbing throughout the entire boat, I'd say your best bet is to drown out the sound of the drips with music until you can make arrangements to sell it."

10. "Looks like someone tried to flush a *Playboy* down the head."

10 Things You Don't Want to Hear from the Exterminator Inspecting Your Boat

1. "I've never seen termites do this much damage in just six months."

3. "Fleas? We didn't treat for fleas, we treated for roaches, ants, spiders, crickets, firebrats, silverfish, sawtoothed grain beetles, Indian meal moths, rice weevils, Mediterranean flour moths, red flour beetles..."

3. While shining a light into the cabin: "Oh, my goodness, look at the size of those buggers."

4. During a termite inspection: "Help! I'm stuck in the engine compartment!"

5. "Dragonflies sometimes get so big around here that they have to call the airport tower for permission to takeoff and land."

6. "Don't worry, the smell of the poison should fade in a few days."

7. "You don't happen to have any antidotes for poison in your boat's first-aid kit, do you?"

8. "You're mistaken. I wasn't dropping roaches, I was bending down to pick them up as specimens."

9. "Your contract covers our placing the mouse traps. It doesn't say anything about emptying them."

10. "If this doesn't work, we're going to have to bomb the boat...and I don't mean with bug spray."

18 Things to Do with a Dead Boat

Planter

Kiddie pool

Bathtub/Hot tub

Tree house

Mother-in-law quarters

Giant beer cooler

Aquarium/Fishing pond

Doghouse

Storage shed

Home office

Natural (on-deck) tanning salon

Mildew research project

Mailbox

Lawn ornament

Fountain

Sandbox

Bird feeder

Outhouse

The Ocean Duchess Would Be Lost...

So you thought that for a change you'd leave the boat driving to someone else and take an exotic cruise, but now find as the shoreline disappears and the seas rise that you don't understand the doublespeak of the captain and crew? The following should help...

What They Say

What They Mean

"Welcome aboard."

"If I wasn't being paid to be here, I wouldn't get on this leaky boat."

"We sail to more exotic destinations than anyone."

"The luggage you had sent ahead could be on any of our twelve ocean liners and is probably having a better time than you are right now."

Sandy Lindsey

What They Say

"The water is a bit " rough today.

"Why don't you settle into a deck chair and relax. We've seen much higher seas than this."

"We hope you're not letting a little thing like the weather bother you."

"If you need anything just let us know."

"In five minutes we'll be showing a movie in the main lounge."

"That noise is nothing to worry about."

What They Mean

"You're going to be banged around so severely that your eyeballs are going to shake right out of their sockets and fall into the lap of the person clutching onto you in terror."

"Clutch onto the person next to you. This ride is going to be more frightening than a Freddy Kruger movie."

"Your fare is nonrefundable."

"Yeah, right. We'll be down below getting seasick, too."

"Just our luck, they sent the *Titanic*. Do you think they were trying to tell us something?"

"Oh no, what was that?"

What They Say	What They Mean
"Will passenger Al-Akmar Khomeni please report to the purser's office. We have just found your missing luggage."	"The mystery noise was a bomb."
"We'll be making a small detour..."	"...to take in water."
"We are now going to have an impromptu lifeboat drill."	"Drill, my foot. Grab your valuables and elbow your fellow guests out of the way, this is as real as it gets. Which is why the captain and crew have already boarded lifeboat number one."
"The management has authorized us to give out coupons good for fifty percent off your next cruise..."	"...just as soon as you all paddle two hundred and fifteen miles to the nearest land."

Fishing in the Afterlife

Did you know that the synonyms for "legendary"—as in he's a "legendary" fisherman—are "mythical" and "fairy tale"? While the antonym is "factual"?

A die-hard fisherman is one who has it written into his will that he's to be buried with his rods and reels. After all these years of trying every new gimmick and technique, deep down he knows that his only chance at landing a Big One is a miracle in Heaven.

Most fishermen have a hard time getting into Heaven. They all stumble when St. Peter asks if they've ever told a lie.

Most fishermen are eventually allowed into Heaven after their lives are reviewed and St. Peter realizes that they've already been through Hell.

Yes, there is fishing in the afterlife. Right there in the Bible it refers to the "weeping and gnashing of teeth."

About the Author

A professional writer and fishing enthusiast, Sandy Lindsey is a regular contributor to *Boating* magazine and has written articles for *WaterSki*, *MidWest Outdoors*, *Angler*, *Sail*, and *Trailer Life/MotorHome*. Lindsey lives in Fort Lauderdale, Florida.